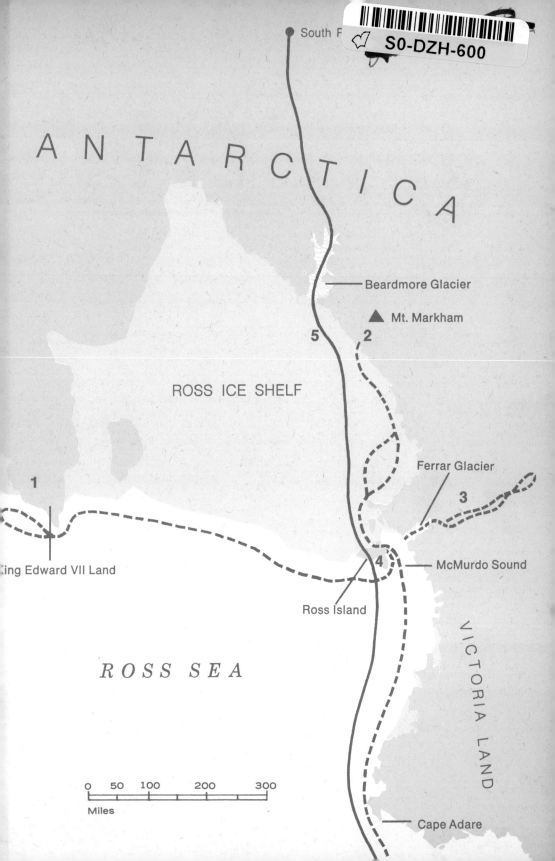

South P[ole]

A N T A R C T I C A

Beardmore Glacier

▲ Mt. Markham

5

2

ROSS ICE SHELF

Ferrar Glacier

1

3

King Edward VII Land

4

McMurdo Sound

Ross Island

VICTORIA LAND

ROSS SEA

0   50   100   200   300

Miles

Cape Adare

THE ASTROLABE, an instrument developed by the Greeks, is the symbol for World Explorer Books. At the time of Columbus, sailors used the astrolabe to chart a ship's course. The arm across the circle could be moved to line up with the sun or a star. Using the number indicated by the pointer, a sailor could tell his approximate location on the sea. Although the astrolabe was not completely accurate, it helped many early explorers in their efforts to conquer the unknown.

World Explorer Books are written especially for children who love adventure and exploration into the unknown. Designed for young readers, each book has been tested by the Dale-Chall readability formula. Leo Fay, Ph.D., Professor of Education at Indiana University, is educational consultant for the series. Dr. Fay, an experienced teacher and lecturer, is well known for his professional bulletins and text material in both elementary reading and social studies.

A WORLD EXPLORER

Robert Falcon Scott

BY JOAN BRISTOW

ILLUSTRATED BY WILLIAM HUTCHINSON

GARRARD PUBLISHING COMPANY
CHAMPAIGN, ILLINOIS

This series is edited by Elizabeth Minot Graves.

Photographs on pages 46, 72, 83, and 87 are from the collections of the Library of Congress.

Contents

1
Up and Over

Robert Falcon Scott, nicknamed Con, stood stiffly at attention on the deck of the training ship *Britannia*. The famous old warship lay moored in the River Dart in Devon, England.

On that spring day of 1880, Con, like the six other boys lined up beside him, was trying to pass the test to join the British navy as a cadet. He was twelve years old and small for his age. His heart pounded with excitement. In the next half hour his future would be decided.

Con stared nervously at the ship's mast. He would soon have to climb up that mast by way of the ladderlike ropes. This was his final test. Con had passed all the other tests. His headmaster at school had given him an excellent report, especially in mathematics. Only this morning the *Britannia's* doctor had said he was in good health. Now he faced a trial of speed and courage.

The captain made a brief signal to the waiting cadet master.

"First boy! Up and over!" barked the cadet master and blew his whistle.

Con watched carefully. The boy was scared and climbed the ropes too fast. At the top he made the mistake of looking down and swayed for a moment with

dizziness. Con nodded to himself. He would not make those mistakes.

Two more boys followed quickly. Then came the order for Con. He raced across the deck, made a leap for the ropes, and climbed like a cat up a tree. Then he took a deep breath, slowed his pace and went up steadily. Before starting down the outside ropes, he stopped for an instant and glanced toward the Devon moorlands. There beyond the trees and hill was his home, a big stone house called Outlands.

Coming down was easy. He dropped to the deck and ran to stand at attention in the line. The grim-faced captain almost smiled.

Con had passed. He was a lucky boy and he knew it, for he would soon be back on the *Britannia* as a cadet. His glance toward Outlands had helped him through the test. Outlands meant home and family—his mother and father, his four sisters, and Archie, his younger brother. They would all be thinking of him today and wishing him luck.

He thought of their fond teasing about his daydreaming and untidy ways. They might call him "Old Mooney" now, but he'd show them.

"No more mooning and daydreaming for me," Scott promised himself. "I'll make my parents proud. I'll be the best officer the navy has."

After three years of training, Con Scott graduated as a full midshipman. He held first-class certificates in mathematics and seamanship and was seventh in his class of twenty-six. Soon he could go to sea in the ships of Her Majesty's Navy, as his grandfather had done before him.

2

The Race

In 1887, four ships of the British navy lay off the island of St. Kitts in the Caribbean Sea. Midshipman Robert Scott, then eighteen years old and serving on the *Rover*, had been busy for the past four years learning how to run a ship. He knew the duties of every seaman aboard. He knew how to reckon the ship's position and how to navigate a course from port to port.

Most exciting of all for Scott had been learning to handle the small boat called a sailing dinghy. This morning he would have a chance to show his skill in a dinghy race. Scott and eleven other boys from the *Rover* got into the ship's longboat and took their places at the oars. "Give way," came the command. Oars flashed in the water as the boys pulled toward the four dinghys waiting in the bay. Longboats from the other ships were headed that way too.

As he rowed, Con glanced up at the *Rover* and saw the captain and his famous guest standing on the ship's bridge. So they would be watching the race!

Each ship had picked one midshipman to compete. Con, chosen by the *Rover*, now stepped from the longboat into his dinghy.

The officer in the longboat called to him, "Don't rush it, Mr. Scott. It's cool and steady wins the race. Do you know your orders?"

Con knew them well. The boys were to sail to a distant flag marker. Then they were to turn, lower sail, row back to the starting point, and tie up.

The starting cannon signaled. *Go!* Con

hauled up the single sail and picked up the wind. The eleven boys waiting in the longboat gave a wild cheer. He was off!

Calmly he judged the best course to the marker. His boat fairly flew over the waves. A gun shot told him he had passed the flag. A second shot warned that another sailboat was close behind.

Now for the long, hard homeward pull.

Scott lowered the sail. Then it was row, row, row until his heart almost burst with the effort. He could hear the second boat pulling closer behind him. Through eyes blinded with sweat, Con caught sight of his finish marker. He gave one extra hard pull. Then the cannon boomed again. Robert Falcon Scott had won the race!

Four nights later, Con was asked to have dinner with the captain and his guest Sir Clements R. Markham, a famous geographer. The midshipmen almost never had dinner with the captain.

Con, stiff in his best uniform, sat next to the important guest. Sir Clements asked Con many questions about his home, his education, and his family. Then he began to talk about his own lifelong interest—the unknown land of Antarctica.

"England really has a claim to the icebound southern continent," Sir Clements said.

He bent toward Scott. "I'm sure you learned in school that England's Captain James Cook was the first to explore Antarctic waters. That was in the 1770s. Then, in 1839, Sir James Clark Ross went to Antarctica and became the first to chart part of its coast."

Turning to the captain, he added, "Our country should be the first to reach the South Pole. It would be a great triumph to cap a long, proud history of exploration."

The captain nodded. "But we've done very little Antarctic exploration since Ross' trip."

"Exactly!" Sir Clements exclaimed. "We should start planning a new polar expedition at once. It may take some years to organize one. I've been making a list of some promising young midshipmen who would be the right age to lead an expedition ten years from now."

When Scott rolled into his hammock on deck late that night, he could not sleep. His thoughts were full of the adventures of the great English explorers —Drake, Raleigh, and Cook. How exciting it must be to sail into the unknown. "Unknown—what a wonderful word," he thought.

3

Who Will Be Leader?

When he was twenty-three, Scott became a lieutenant. He had the highest mark in seamanship of all the young men who graduated from the officers' school that year. Then in an exam given by the Royal Naval College he ranked first.

Eager to rise higher in the ranks of the navy, Scott applied and was accepted for training at torpedo school. The handsome, serious young officer became an expert in the use of this new weapon. Within three years he was a torpedo lieutenant.

The promotion gave him higher pay. Scott, always careful and quiet, began to spend a little money to have fun. Then he learned that his father had been forced to sell his business, and the money from its sale was almost gone. Mr. and Mrs. Scott were close to poverty. So Scott knew he must help them. His own fun would have to wait.

Con's brother and sisters had left home. One sister became a nurse, another went on the stage, and two opened a dress-making shop in London. Archie went to Africa with the British army. The two sons sent home money to care for their parents.

In a few years Mr. Scott died. Then,

not long afterward, typhoid fever killed Con's beloved brother, Archie. Now Con alone had to support his mother.

In 1897 Torpedo Lieutenant Scott was on the *Empress of India*, docked at a naval base. There he again met Sir Clements Markham, now president of the Royal Geographical Society. Markham remembered the midshipman who had won the dinghy race at St. Kitts. He was pleased to learn from the other officers that Scott had become a fine commander of men, as well as a skilled navigator and surveyor.

"I'm still hopeful that an English party will explore Antarctica," Markham told Scott. He had completed the list of young officers who might lead such a group. He did not tell Scott that his name was high on the list.

"This expedition must explore on land," Markham went on. "Ross tried to find a waterway into the Antarctic continent, but his ship was stopped by a wall of ice. Even if such a waterway is there, it is no doubt frozen over. We must land and explore on foot."

Scott listened with interest. However, nearly three years passed before the two men talked again. Scott, now 31, happened to meet Sir Clements on a London street.

To Scott's surprise Markham said, "I was about to write you. Come along to my club. I have exciting news."

When they were settled with a cup of tea, Markham said eagerly, "Scott, several countries want to explore Antarctica now. People here are interested too—they don't want England to be left behind. Plans for a British expedition are well under way. Here, look at these."

The papers Markham handed to Scott explained the plan. The two groups were working together to organize the trip. The Royal Geographical Society wanted to map the Antarctic continent and learn more about the ice wall that had stopped Ross' explorations. The Royal Society, a

group of scientists, wanted to study the weather and magnetism in Antarctica. They were also interested in minerals, plants, and animal life of the polar region. Many people hoped the expedition would be able to plant the British flag at the South Pole.

"In summer the ice in the polar sea melts into chunks. Then a ship can sail in close to the land," Markham said to Scott.

"However, the polar summer is very short. By the time a camp is built on shore, it will be too cold and stormy to do much exploring. The men will have to winter over in the camp and on shipboard, then start inland the following spring.

"As you know, that close to the Pole the sun is completely out of sight during the winter months. The temperature stays way below zero. Bitter winds blow all the time. It's not safe to leave shelter for long."

As Sir Clements described the hard challenge of the icebound land, Scott began to share his excitement.

"It is most important to choose the right man to lead the expedition," said Markham. Scott agreed.

"I think you are that man. Why don't you apply for the command?" Markham said suddenly.

Scott was stunned. What an adventure! He longed to go, but he had to think of his mother.

When he asked his mother's advice, she firmly answered, "Go!"

Scott applied for the job, and one year later the command was his.

4

The *Discovery* Sails

All the next year Scott worked hard setting up the expedition. His tiny office was piled high with warm boots, camp stoves, and samples of dried food as he tested and ordered supplies.

Together Scott and Markham went to Norway to visit Fridtjof Nansen, a famous polar explorer. Nansen showed his guests the tents, skis, sledges, and clothing he had used exploring the Arctic.

He warned Scott, "Sudden storms, hidden ice cracks, and a hundred other dangers may trap the polar explorer. Norwegians are used to long, hard winters. We learn about these dangers as children. How can Englishmen, who see so little snow, know how to keep alive in the Antarctic?"

Scott was not discouraged. He liked testing himself with hard jobs. "Englishmen have always been explorers," he said to Sir Clements on the way home. "We may not have polar experience, but we do have the courage and the will. That's what counts."

Back in England Scott began choosing the 47 men best fitted to share his great adventure. He quickly decided on a doctor, Dr. Edward Wilson, who was also an artist and zoologist. Dr. Wilson's quiet manner and wise advice soon made him Scott's favorite.

As his second-in-command, Scott picked Ernest Shackleton, a tough officer of the merchant marine. He chose nine scientists with different skills. Many of the rest of the crew were young navy men.

Meanwhile Sir Clements had been very busy raising money. The government gave some; interested individuals gave more. With some of the money Scott paid for a specially planned wooden ship to be built in Scotland. He went there again and again to see that every part was right.

When workmen laughed at its strange shape, Scott explained, "It may look odd, but that heavy round bottom could save our lives. It won't be crushed by pressure from huge ice chunks."

At last, on August 5, 1901, the ship was

loaded and waiting at Cowes, a port in southern England. King Edward and Queen Alexandra came aboard to wish the expedition farewell. The king presented Scott with a medal. Scott's mother proudly pinned it on her son's uniform.

Horns tooted and crowds cheered as the ship, named the *Discovery*, steamed out of the harbor. A thrill of excitement swept over Scott as he felt the ship rise and fall on the waves. He was back on the open sea. He was in command of an expedition and headed for the unknown! Yet, as always, he worried. Had he thought of everything? Was he strong enough for the tests ahead? Would the trip bring triumph or defeat?

The wide, heavy ship was slow. It had to stop in South Africa for fuel. At another stop, in New Zealand, Scott picked

up fresh food and the Siberian dogs he
had ordered. These dogs would be used
to pull the heavy sleds, called sledges,
through the snow.

It was not until late December that the
Discovery was pushing her way through
the ice chunks in the Antarctic Ocean.
The sun slowly circled overhead in the
endless daylight of the polar summer.
Scott spent hours at the ship's rail watch-

ing the sleepy seals and the comical penguins sitting on the passing ice chunks.

Part of Scott's job was to keep a daily record of the trip. One bright night he was working on this diary when he heard the cry, "Land in sight!"

He rushed on deck to join the excited crew. There, white and silent in the distance, lay the Antarctic continent. Scott gazed in wonder at this land of mystery

—the land he must conquer, the mystery he must solve.

The men were buzzing with talk the next morning at breakfast. Scott rose to speak.

"Gentlemen, at last our work can begin. Cape Adare, which lies just ahead, is at the northern end of Victoria Land. We are to chart the entire coast of this land. At the far end, we will come to the Ross Sea. Here we should find the great wall of ice that stopped Ross' exploration. We'll chart the wall and try to find out if it rests on land or water.

"As we sail along, I'll watch for a sheltered spot for a camp. We must be settled before the water freezes over for the winter."

Scott stopped the ship at several points to set up bright red cans with messages inside them. Next summer a relief ship would come with supplies and would follow those small red signs of Scott's route.

As the *Discovery* moved south, icebergs bigger than tall buildings drifted into her path. Pulled by strong currents, blocked by heavy ice chunks, the little ship often came within inches of a fatal crash. The crew stood alert, quick to follow their captain's orders. They had great faith in his skill. Again and again, the ship twisted away from danger.

Scott steered the ship into the safety of McMurdo Sound at the western end of the Ross Sea. He went ashore and climbed a small hill on Ross Island. Behind him stood Mt. Erebus, a dark, steaming volcano. To the west lay the blue waters of the sound and the snow-covered mountains of Victoria Land. To the south was a great plain of glittering ice, the surface of the Ross Ice Barrier.

"Ross Island is a perfect spot for our camp!" Scott exclaimed. "It has a good harbor and mountains to protect us!"

Steaming, or sailing when possible to save coal, the *Discovery* followed the edge of the barrier. The dazzling blue and white wall of ice sometimes rose 200 feet above them.

Wilson spent days sketching it. Every few hours the scientists measured the depth of the ocean. They decided there was no land beneath the ice wall. It was a huge shelf of ice covering part of the Ross Sea.

On January 29, the *Discovery* passed the point where Ross had turned his ship around. They were now exploring a part of the vast ice wall that had not been

seen or charted before. "Keep a sharp eye to the east. Ross thought he saw land in that direction," Scott told the crew.

The next day Shackleton said doubtfully, "Are those dark patches ahead land or clouds?" All telescopes turned toward the dark spots. Then Scott cried, "We've found new land!"

They had come to the eastern end of the Ross Ice Shelf and the Ross Sea. Scott named the land he had discovered King Edward VII Land.

A few more days of sailing took them 150 miles along the unexplored coast. Scott wanted to go farther, but he knew the winter freeze would soon begin. This rocky shore offered no safe harbor. So Scott ordered the ship to head back for the spot he'd found in McMurdo Sound. Here, on February 8, he dropped anchor.

5

The First Winter

At the end of April, spring flowers bloomed on the other side of the world in England. But in the Antarctic the four-month winter began. The *Discovery* was now frozen into the ice close to Ross Island.

Both the ship and the snug base hut on shore hummed with activity.

On the ship the sewing machine clattered; warm, windproof clothes were being made for the spring trips. Hammers

banged on the metal sledge runners; they must be smooth and strong. In a corner big Lieutenant Evans pounded out spikes for the ice boots.

Working on papers piled on a desk in the middle, Scott kept an eye on everything.

"Hard work will keep us healthy and happy," Scott said to Wilson, "and there is plenty of it to do."

Wilson smiled. "We've done a lot in the past three months. Why, we ski and handle the dogs almost like experts now. To think that most of us never saw skis or sledges before!"

"Yes, we've learned a great deal," Scott agreed, "but we've made mistakes, fatal mistakes."

He frowned, thinking of the men he had sent to set up a can with a message for the relief ship. When a storm blew up, they still kept traveling. One young seaman, blinded by the swirling snow, slipped over an icy cliff to his death in the sea.

"Each time I've sent a party to try out the dogs and sledges," Scott went on, "the trip failed in some way. We must change our equipment and improve it. And we must learn to load the sledges better."

Scott glanced up as an icy blast swept through the opened door. Lashley had gone out to the weather station which had been set up. Temperature and wind speed had to be checked every few hours.

"At least it's good to see the scientific work going so well," Wilson said.

Earlier the scientists had collected tiny sea animals. Now by the dim light of oil lamps, they spent long hours over their microscopes examining their collection. Other scientists worked in a special unheated hut, recording magnetism. They were close to the magnetic pole and knew that polar weather and magnetism affect the rest of the world. Scott watched these records carefully. "This may be the most important work we do," he said.

To keep everyone happy, Scott planned evenings of entertainment for the men. There were parties with gay paper chains and carved ice decorations. The scientists gave talks, and the men put on shows. Shackleton even produced a newspaper, *The South Polar Times.*

When the sun returned, Scott and Shackleton were eager for a last test run with the sledges before they started on the long exploring trip south.

"It's safer to travel with a group of three. We'll take another man with us," Scott told Shackleton.

On the first night out, Scott and his companions were very tired. They did not take time to set up their tent firmly. Near dawn Scott woke and lifted the flap of his sleeping bag. "What's happened?" he mumbled.

He was alone in the snow, with an icy wind whipping his face. "I must have rolled out of the tent in my sleep," he realized. Now, more awake, he looked about and saw a side of the tent flapping wildly nearby. A gale had come up during the night.

"Shackleton! Barne! Grab the edge of the tent!" Scott shouted. "It's about to blow away." He crawled through a drift and caught at the canvas.

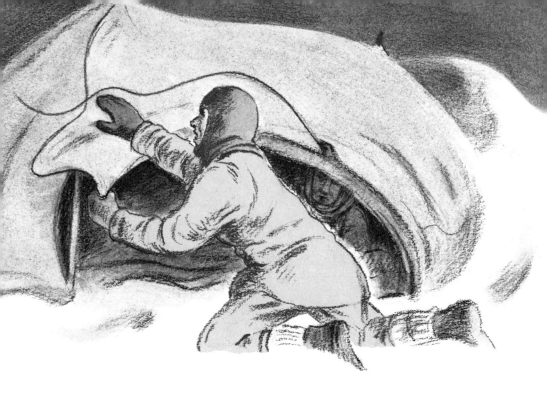

The wind tore at their shelter for a full day. Their fingers were freezing, but they did not dare let go of the tent. Finally in the evening the wind died down. Rubbing his frostbitten fingers, Scott said, "Is there no end to the hard lessons we must learn?"

However, by the time they returned to camp after two weeks of travel, Scott thought they knew their jobs well.

6

Farthest South

Five neatly packed sledges stood ready at the base camp on the spring morning of November 2, 1902. Scott, Wilson, and Shackleton were starting south to explore the land of Antarctica.

The still air rang with excited shouts and laughter. The nineteen dogs caught the gay mood. Barking and straining against their harnesses, they set off at a brisk trot.

Scott, driving a sledge, led the way to the ice shelf that lay over the Ross Sea. He turned with a bright smile and waved a last good-bye to the cheering men who were to stay behind. Some of them would explore in other directions while he was gone.

"We will travel south only as far as food and strength will allow," Scott said. However, each of the three men secretly hoped to reach the South Pole.

Within a day they caught up with and traveled near the support party that had gone ahead carrying extra supplies. The explorers could not carry enough food for the entire trip south and back. The support parties were leaving piles of food and oil along part of the way. Each pile, or depot, was marked with a black flag and a high mound of snow, called a cairn.

The supplies would be waiting for the three explorers to use as they traveled back to camp.

"We'll stay on the flat ice shelf as long as possible," Scott told the men. "I don't know how far south it goes, but it should be easy to travel on it. The land to the west seems to be only mountains."

Scott daily observed the sun to reckon their position. He kept a record of the distance and direction of each march. After ten days, he could no longer see the mountains to the west.

On November 15, Scott called the support party together. "You must return to camp," he ordered, "while you still have enough food for the trip."

Now Scott and his two companions were alone in the vast white unknown. Only the hiss of the sledge runners and the patter of the dogs' feet broke the empty silence.

Scott was upset to see the dogs beginning to weaken. Their supply of dried fish had spoiled and made them sick.

When Scott's most faithful dog slipped and fell, Scott gently lifted him to a comfortable spot on the sledge. "We'll help pull the sledges now," he told Wilson and Shackleton.

The summer sun softened the snow, and the sledge runners stuck on the surface. Even worse, they often sank deep into it. The men and dogs struggled to travel a few feet. Some days they covered less than four miles in nine hours. One by one the weakened dogs began to die.

"How much more of this can we live through?" Scott wondered secretly.

Two weeks later he saw the faint

Robert Falcon Scott, on his skis in Antarctica, at left. Below, men pull a packed sledge over the rough ice.

outlines of distant mountains and began to feel more hopeful. Each day there were new· headlands and peaks to add to his map. Once again there was the thrill of discovery.

Christmas Day dawned clear and calm. A good eleven-mile march added to their holiday mood. That evening, they sat on their rolled-up sleeping bags around the tiny camp stove. They made cocoa and a warm mixture of grain and meat called "hoosh." Double helpings and a bit of chocolate seemed like a banquet.

"Still, I could do with a bit of my mum's plum pudding," said Shackleton.

Scott grinned in contentment. "For once though, we aren't as hungry after dinner as we were before it."

Constant hunger was only part of their suffering. Their faces and lips were badly cracked and dry from the wind. The glare of the sun on the snow made their eyes burn. Even worse, the men's feet were beginning to swell from scurvy, a disease caused by lack of fresh food.

However, the excitement of discovery and the honor of England meant more to them than their pain.

On the last day of the year they saw a snow-covered cape blocking their way to the south. Beyond were huge twin mountain peaks. "I'm going to name them for Sir Clements Markham," Scott said.

Scott longed to explore farther, but he soberly faced the facts. They could not hope to reach the Pole. It was still more than 400 miles away. Only nine dogs were left, and the food supply was low. Furthermore, Shackleton's scurvy was worse.

Sadly Scott said, "We must turn back."

Blinding storms whipped them day after day now. When the last of the dogs died, Scott was relieved. "I prefer to pull the sledges myself," he said. "The poor beasts should never be made to suffer so."

Because of the stormy weather, it took longer to travel from one supply depot to the next. The men were starving, and Shackleton was very weak. He coughed, choked, and staggered along in a daze.

Shackleton was determined to continue to share the work. Finally Scott had to command him to stop. They fitted a sail on a sledge, and Shackleton rode. The trip became a race to save Shackleton's life.

What relief Scott felt when they reached McMurdo Sound on February 3. What a joy to see the *Discovery!* The ship was gay with fresh paint and bright flags to welcome their return.

7

Victoria Land

"It's the captain! They've made it!" The crew rushed out to greet the ragged men and to help Shackleton, now making his painful way on skis.

Scott was proud that they had traveled 960 miles in 93 days. They had suffered cruel hardships and lived. They had made maps of much new land and found the southwestern end of the Ross Sea.

Shackleton was put to bed, and Scott went off to have a hot bath which he called "delicious." Then a crewman came

in to say, "Captain Colbeck of the *Morning* to see you, sir."

The relief ship *Morning* had arrived a few days before and was sitting ten miles away in the open water. She had brought news, mail, and supplies. Scott couldn't decide which was most welcome.

Scott had expected the summer sun to melt the ice which was holding the *Discovery* fast. But the ship was still frozen in solid ice. "The days are growing colder," Scott said. "The ice will not melt this year. The *Morning* is also in danger of freezing in."

Quickly the crew moved tons of supplies from the *Morning* across the sea ice to the *Discovery*. Then the *Morning* sailed away. With her went eight men who wanted to go home and also Shackleton who was too ill to remain in the Antarctic.

The men of the *Discovery* happily settled in for another dark, busy winter.

Scott began preparing for a new trip. "I want to see what lies beyond the high mountains here at the edge of Victoria Land," he told the men.

Ferrar, the geologist, had explored a glacier that cut between the mountain peaks. Glaciers are like huge rivers of ice that move a few inches each year, cutting valleys as they go.

"The glacier's surface is broken by cracks, or crevasses, in many places," Ferrar said. "Even so, it's the best path over the mountains."

When spring came, Scott led a party of eleven men toward Ferrar's glacier. He set a fast pace as he climbed up huge snow ridges and around heaps of fallen ice chunks.

"Look at that crevasse. It's wide as a city street," he called back to the men panting behind him. Slowing a little, he led them over a narrow bridge of ice which crossed the gap. "Don't look down," he warned. "There's a hundred feet of empty space between you and the bottom of that crack."

On a steep slope near the top of the glacier, the party was caught by a sudden storm. Scott saw one tiny level spot. The men dashed for it and chopped a place to set up tents. For six days the wind howled and the flapping canvas thundered above their heads.

The men, cramped in the tents, were getting sick and restless. Their sleeping bags were stiff with ice, and they could not sleep. Scott said, "Storm or no storm, tomorrow we'll go on climbing."

Freed from their snowy prison, the men climbed recklessly. Their one thought was to get away from that awful spot. The following day came the cry, "We've done it! We're over the mountains!"

Ahead stretched an endless flat white plain. Scott's instruments showed that they were a mile and a half above sea level. "If the plain stays at this high level all the way to the other coast of Antarctica," Scott said, "this is the highest continent in the world."

The men had made several depots of food and supplies on the glacier. Now they made their last one. Then Scott sent six men back to the ship.

Scott and a team of men plodded westward across the icy plain. No living thing or new shape broke the flatness. The view never changed. The wind never stopped.

Though Scott was the oldest man on the team, he was the strongest. If the other men felt tired, they tried to hide it. "If he can do it, I can too," one man kept saying. "My legs are as long as his."

However, Scott saw that three men were getting weak. "For the safety of all," he told them, "I must send you back."

Scott, Lashley, and Evans moved on alone dragging only one sledge. Scott had decided they would travel west until November 30. When that day came, the end of the icy plain still was not in sight. In the dim light of the tent that night, he wrote, "We have made our last outward march, thank heaven."

The book Scott needed to figure out their position had been lost in a storm. He believed they had traveled 300 miles from the ship, but he could not be sure.

Without his book Scott could only guess at the direction of the supply depots on the return trip. When they reached the top of the glacier, he was uncertain where the next supply depot was.

As they edged down the ice, Lashley suddenly slipped and flew down the slope on his back. All three men were hooked to the sledge by long leather ropes, called traces. When Lashley fell, he pulled the sledge and the other men after him.

Shooting along the ice, they hit bumps and were thrown high into the air. Rough snow stopped them at last. Hurting from head to toe, Scott looked around in a daze. Suddenly he spotted a frozen waterfall that he knew was near a depot! They were no longer lost.

Later, almost within sight of base camp, the men came close to death again. Scott

and Evans were pulling the sledge, and Lashley was walking behind.

All at once Scott felt the snow give beneath his feet. He dropped into space, then stopped with a jerk, dangling by his leather harness. He had stepped into a crevasse hidden beneath the snow. The bottom was hundreds of feet below. Evans hung helplessly above him.

Scott called, "Evans, are you all right?"

"Perfectly fine, sir," was the quiet reply.

The sledge, Scott could see, was bridging the crevasse. Lashley had caught the back of it as they fell. He had dug his heels into the snow and was holding the sledge with all his strength.

Slowly Scott reached up to grab the leather rope from which he hung. Hand over hand he dragged his painfully bruised body upward. His freezing fingers slid on the rope, but with a last mighty pull he reached the top of the crevasse.

"I couldn't have held on much longer," Lashley groaned with relief. Quickly the two men pulled Evans up and got under way again.

In a few days they were back at the ship. Warm food, baths, and beds seemed fit for a king.

A few weeks later, in January 1904, the relief ship *Morning* returned to McMurdo Sound. With her came the whaling ship *Terra Nova*.

"The navy commands you to return to England," the officers told Scott. "If the *Discovery* cannot be freed from the ice, you must sail home with us."

"The *Discovery* has been our home for two years. We can't go without her," Scott said stubbornly. The men agreed.

Officers and men worked night and day with saws and dynamite to break the ice around the ship. One final blast of dynamite jolted the *Discovery* out of her trap. She floated free in the open blue water once again.

With a last sad look toward their tiny hut, Scott called, "Full speed ahead!" The *Discovery* and her crew were headed back to civilization.

8

Home and Fame

When the *Discovery* reached England, small boats of every kind crowded the harbor to welcome the explorers home. Scott found that he was famous. He had made maps of a large part of the Antarctic coast and the Ross Ice Shelf. He had discovered King Edward VII Land and many mountains. He had explored 300 miles inland on the Antarctic continent and brought back enough scientific information to fill twelve big books. He had gone closer to the South Pole than any man before. He was a hero.

Scott was the guest of the king for a week at Balmoral Castle. He received praise, medals, and honors from scientific groups at home and abroad. The navy gave him the rank of captain. He had six months' leave to make speeches and write his book, *The Voyage of the Discovery*. He was invited to endless parties.

Scott did not care for social life. After two years he was glad to be called back to sea duty. He liked the dangers of the sea. He enjoyed the challenge of commanding great ships. Yet Scott longed for even greater tests of strength and courage. He dreamt of the South Pole.

Scott knew that it would be hard to get money for a new expedition. Many Englishmen had lost interest when no great wealth was found in the Antarctic.

Then to Scott's surprise, Shackleton announced plans for his own trip to Antarctica. Scott knew Shackleton had been given money by a few people who were still interested. So Scott had no hope of getting money, but he longed to prepare an expedition himself. He could think of nothing else.

Then, at just this time, Scott found a new interest. He met Kathleen Bruce.

Scott immediately liked the tall dark-haired girl with lively blue eyes. She was a talented sculptress who enjoyed working and living alone in London. Her independence and joy of life delighted the serious-minded captain. Scott fell deeply in love.

A captain's pay was enough to support both his mother and a wife. In September 1908, Scott and Kathleen were married.

That same year, Shackleton led his expedition to Antarctica. He explored the polar plateau and beat Scott's "farthest south" record by 366 miles. When he returned to England in June 1909, cheering crowds greeted him. Scott, now on shore duty in London, joined the crowd unnoticed. Later he went to meet the new hero and shake his hand.

Scott described the scene to Kathleen. "Still, he didn't make it to the Pole," he said.

"Con, that honor should be yours," Kathleen cried. "Somehow you must go to the Pole yourself!"

Scott smiled at his strong-minded wife. "It's not that easy. An expedition costs money, and I'm not the only one who wants to reach the Pole. Many countries are interested now."

In September news came that Robert E. Peary of the United States had reached the North Pole.

"An Englishman *must* be the first to reach the South Pole!" Scott told Kathleen. "There's no time to lose. The Norwegian explorer, Roald Amundsen, has been getting ready to go to the North Pole. Now that Peary has beaten him there, Amundsen may head south instead."

September 1909 was a very important month for the Scotts. On the 14th their son, Peter Markham Scott, was born. The very next day Scott announced plans for a new Antarctic expedition. His first goal was to reach the South Pole, but scientific study would be important too. He would take the best scientific equipment along with him.

Scott went from city to city giving speeches and asking for money for the expedition. He hated this work, and the money came in slowly. Then one night he came home waving a newspaper.

"Kathleen, look! Peary announces that he is going south to the Pole. He calls it a race with the British. Our people will never let another country be first. Now we'll get money."

Scott's preparations moved quickly. He bought the old whaling ship *Terra Nova* and had her made ready. Of the 8,000 men who wanted to join him, Scott chose the best. He asked his trusted friend Dr. Wilson to head the scientific staff.

Ordering supplies was easy this time. Scott knew what he needed. He enjoyed choosing among the new inventions of the day.

"The telephone will be useful," he told Wilson. "Color film and movie cameras will show the beauty of the place. Best of the inventions is the gasoline engine. I have been working to help build a sledge with an engine. If it is successful, we can explore twice as far as before."

Scott ordered 31 dogs, but he had little faith in them. He was convinced that ponies would be best for pulling heavy loads through the snow. He planned to pick up seventeen Russian ponies and their two drivers in New Zealand.

On June 15, 1910, the *Terra Nova* left England, with Lieutenant E. R. G. R. Evans, Scott's second-in-command, acting as captain. Scott and Kathleen followed as passengers on another ship. They planned to meet the *Terra Nova* in Australia.

9

Back to Antarctica

"Am going south. Amundsen." These were the words on a telegram handed to Scott when he reached Australia. The Norwegian explorer intended to make it a race for the Pole!

"Any attempt to race will ruin our plans," Scott told Wilson. "The proper as well as the wiser thing for us is to go ahead as though this had not happened."

"Of course," Wilson agreed. "You cannot risk men's lives or give up our scientific studies."

Kathleen tried to comfort Scott. "At least Peary gave up his plans. You might have had two challengers."

However, thoughts of his Norwegian rival were never far from Scott's mind. Amundsen was an experienced polar explorer. He had made several trips to the Arctic and had discovered the Northwest Passage. But he had no scientific interests. He had only one purpose—to reach the South Pole first.

After a long final stop in New Zealand, Scott's ship was ready to sail for Antarctica on November 29. Kathleen and Scott said a loving good-bye before he left for the dock. There newspapermen crowded around him.

"What are your chances for getting to the Pole?" one reporter asked.

"We may get through; we may not. It is all a matter of luck," Scott replied.

From beginning to end, luck was the one thing this expedition did not bring to Scott.

Rough seas and heavy ice chunks often slowed the ship. Scott paced the deck impatiently. "Before winter we must build

Siberian dogs sprawl on the crowded deck of the *Terra Nova*. They were brought to pull sledges of supplies on some expeditions.

our camp and lay supply depots for the spring trip south," he said worriedly. "We haven't much time."

On January 5, 1911, the ship anchored off the shore of Ross Island in McMurdo Sound. A big new hut quickly rose on the black sand below Mt. Erebus. The old hut, fifteen miles to the south, made an outpost camp.

Scott was delighted with the new base camp. "We'll have all the comforts of home when the *Terra Nova* goes back to New Zealand," he said.

Then bad luck struck again. A motor sledge crashed through some soft ice and was lost at the bottom of the sea.

The depot-laying trip was also disappointing. They had to move very slowly. Captain Oates, who was taking care of the ponies, came to Scott. "Sir, the ponies are too heavy for this soft snow. They sink in and have to struggle to get free. The poor things are worn out."

"Yes," Scott agreed. "We'll never get the depots as far south as I'd hoped." Finally, Scott ordered the men to dump the last supplies. He had wanted to go 36 miles farther. How differently the trip would have ended if "One Ton Depot" had been farther south.

There was more trouble on the return trip. Scott was driving a dog sledge late one night. Suddenly some of the dogs in his team dropped out of sight. A crevasse! Scott peered down the great crack. Ten dogs were dangling helplessly in their harnesses. Two others had slipped out of their harnesses and fallen to an ice bridge 65 feet below.

The ten dogs were hauled to safety.

How could Scott rescue the other two? He made a daring decision. "Bring a rope!" he called. He had himself lowered down to the narrow bridge. He tied the rope first to one dog, then the other. He stood balancing on the slippery bridge until the dogs were pulled up. Then he was hauled to safety too.

When they got to the camp, Scott was given unhappy news. The *Terra Nova* had gone to explore King Edward VII Land. On the way, Captain Campbell had sailed into the Bay of Whales. There he found Amundsen's camp.

The rival Antarctic explorer and his eight men were already hard at work training 130 dogs for a trip to the Pole.

Scott had known that Amundsen was somewhere in the Antarctic. Still he was upset by the news. "He's closer to the Pole than we are," Scott admitted to Wilson. "Our 30 dogs can't match his 130. But the ponies are stronger again, and we have the motor sledges. We still have a chance!"

Scott spoke to the men. "We have to complete our trips to study the penguin colonies. And there are minerals and sea life specimens to collect before winter. We must forget about Amundsen."

10

The Race Is On

On the spring morning of November 1, Scott moved briskly among the men and animals.

"Let the fast ponies lead out; now bring along the slow ones," he called. "You men with the dog sledges keep well behind."

Scott slid forward on his skis into the lead. The small parade of fourteen men, two dog teams, and a string of ponies began the hard push south for the Pole.

Scott could not know that Amundsen had made his start for the same goal several days before. Yet he was certain that somewhere in the great white wilderness, his rival was racing to win the honor Scott wanted for England.

Once again Scott's party would move south across the ice shelf. After 400 miles, they would cut up through the mountains to the central plateau. They planned to climb Beardmore Glacier, discovered by Shackleton on his expedition.

The motor sledges had started several days ahead of the main party. "If they work, we cannot fail to win the race," Scott told Wilson. But in less than a week he found them sitting empty in the snow. Both motors had burned out. The drivers were pulling the heavy loads themselves.

For a month Scott and his support parties traveled about ten miles each day.
The surface of the ice shelf was often
like the frozen waves of a stormy sea.
These waves, called *sastrugi*, held soft
snow in their hollows. In the struggle to
cross them, three ponies weakened and
died.

On December 5, Scott said hopefully,
"Just one day's march to the base of
Beardmore Glacier. Our supplies are good,
and our health is good. Maybe our luck
has changed."

That night a heavy storm piled deep
snow on the camp. Scott watched helplessly as the snow changed to sleet. They
could not travel in such weather. "Could
Amundsen's luck be as bad as this?" he
wondered.

Wind-driven rain poured into the tents

and soaked sleeping bags and clothing. The dogs curled up comfortably under the snow. But the ponies stood shivering in a shelter Captain Oates had tried to build for them. Their coats and manes were crusted with ice.

One of the men made up a verse:

The snow is all melting
and everything's afloat,
If this goes on much longer we'll have to
turn the tent upside down
And use it as a boat.

After four wet days, the rain stopped, and the party moved on. They had to wade through slush eighteen inches deep. This was too much for the weary ponies. They all died that night.

Still Scott felt better when they reached the mountains. Red and black cliffs stood high near Beardmore Glacier. "What a nice change to see color after all the weeks of sparkling white," he said.

With a hearty "One, two, three, together," Scott gave a yank on his sledge. The party began the long pull up the mountain pass.

Often they could not keep a foothold on the rippled ice and fell with painful thuds. Sometimes the glacier was a network of hidden crevasses. Then man after man fell from sight and was caught with a jerk at the end of his leather rope. Often fog trapped them for hours.

Scott mapped the mountain as they climbed slowly upward. Supply depots were left at several places. Then when they were near the top, the weary dog teams were sent back to camp with the weakest members of the support party.

Huge ice masses on Antarctica tower over the
men and dogs of Scott's expedition.

At last on Christmas Day, two tiny green tents were sitting at the very top of the glacier. The air on the high plateau was thin, and the temperature was 40 degrees below zero. Breathing was painful and difficult. Only Lieutenant Bowers didn't seem to mind the cold and was happy outside the tent doing camp chores.

On January 3, a final depot was built on the Polar Plateau. Then the last of the support party started back toward the base camp.

Five men were to head for the Pole. Wilson, Petty Officer Edgar Evans, and Captain Lawrence Oates had been picked first. At the last minute Scott decided to take sturdy little Bowers too.

Bowers had left his skis at a depot on the glacier, and food had been planned for only four men. But Henry Bowers was the best at packing the sledges. "We just couldn't get on without you," Scott told him.

The new year brought no new luck. The weather stayed very cold. Winds blew night and day. The men slid and fell as they dragged the sledge over the high waves of frozen snow. In spite of the hardships, their excitement grew as each day's struggle brought them closer to the Pole.

On January 15, Scott felt safe to say, "Boys, we cannot fail now. Two good days of marching will get us to the Pole."

In two days his dream would come true —if only Amundsen had not reached the Pole before him.

Next morning Scott, as always, was impatient to be moving on. He hurried the others to an early start. After two hours, Bowers' keen eyes spotted a black dot on the horizon.

"Perhaps it's only a mound of ice," he said hopefully. Next they saw ski marks and dog tracks. Then a tent and flag came into view. The flag of Norway was flying at the Pole!

The men had tried to be cheerful during the long hard months of the march. Now they could no longer pretend. They looked in silence at the winning flag.

In Amundsen's tent Scott found a letter to the king of Norway. A note for Scott invited him to use the supplies that had been left behind. He was also asked to deliver the king's letter in case Amundsen did not get back home. The notes were dated December 15. Amundsen had been at the Pole a full month before Scott.

Grimly Scott said, "Well, we must do what we have come to do." The men located the Pole exactly and set up the British flag. They took pictures of themselves. Then hurriedly they left the place that now seemed to them the worst place in the world.

Unable to smile, the tired and weather-beaten English explorers pose at the Pole. Captain Scott is standing at left.

11

The South Pole

Scott knew that the return trip would be hard. Hope had carried the tired men through more than two months of bitter suffering. Now hope was gone.

The 21-day march over the windswept plateau was harder than before. The men grew weak, and signs of scurvy appeared.

At a rest stop Scott took Wilson aside. "I don't like the look of Evans," he said. "The frostbite on his hand isn't healing as it should. He isn't pulling well either."

Wilson agreed. "Yes, he seems confused. He may have injured his brain in that bad fall a few days ago."

When they reached the glacier, the air was warmer. The men stopped to hunt for minerals. Wilson was excited by his find of a rock with a clear fossil print of a leaf and stem.

Examining it, Scott said, "This rock alone makes our trip worthwhile. It proves, as we had guessed, that this continent once had a warm climate. It is hard to believe that trees and flowers once grew on this cold, bare mountain."

Part way down the glacier, Scott found himself in a network of wide crevasses. He turned this way and that hunting for an escape. This increased the time between depots, and food ran short.

Evans grew worse and could no longer

help with camp work. Near the bottom of the glacier he dropped behind the group. "We must ski back for him," Scott told the others. They found Evans on his knees, wild-eyed and unable to walk. That night he died.

The sad little party grew more and more tired. Each day's march was shorter. In the blowing snow, often Scott could not see the cairns marking the depots.

At each depot Scott became more worried. He found food, but the fuel oil cans had leaked. There was barely enough oil to heat one meal a day. Warm food would keep the men alive, but cold, dry biscuits would not.

Blow followed blow. The heaviest storms of autumn began. The surface of the ice shelf was rough and sticky. A long day of straining to pull the sledge never took them more than six miles. The hungry men grew weaker.

Scott could see that Oates' frostbitten feet and scurvy made walking very painful for him. Oates did not complain, but he knew he could not walk much farther. He realized that he was slowing the march and begged to be left behind.

Scott would not let him give up. "Keep plugging along. You'll make it."

Early on the morning of March 16, Oates decided what he must do. He said, "I am just going outside and may be [gone] some time." He stepped out of the tent into a blizzard and was never seen again. Oates had given his life to save the others.

Five days later Scott checked their location. "We're just eleven miles from One Ton Depot," he said.

"What a feast we'll have there," Bowers answered. "We'll have plenty of food for the rest of the trip too."

Then the wind began to roar, whipping the snow in blinding swirls. A storm held the men inside their tent. They had very little food, and only enough oil to heat one more meal.

Each day Scott hoped that one man could go ahead on skis and bring back food and oil. Each day the storm raged on. The three men knew the end was near, but they talked of home and the future. They were determined to die bravely.

Scott wrote letters to those he loved most—his wife, with a special message about his son, and his mother. He wrote a statement for the public and letters to his friends.

After eight days the storm ended. Wilson and Bowers lay on either side of Scott in a sleep close to death. Scott forced his dying mind and fingers to write: "March 29, 1912: We shall stick it out to the end, but we are getting weaker of course, and the end cannot be far.

"It seems a pity, but I do not think I can write more. R. Scott."

"Last entry: For God's sake look after our people."

12

Afterword

The *Terra Nova* returned to McMurdo Sound and waited for the Polar party, now long overdue. When winter storms and darkness ended in October, a group set out to search for Scott.

Ten miles south of One Ton Depot, one of the men saw a dark patch in the distance. He skied over to it. The top six inches of a tent showed above the snow.

Silently the party gathered to look at

the find. Would the tent be empty, or was this the frozen grave of their lost companions? They dug the snow away and opened the tent. There was the body of Wilson, his hands clasped on his chest. Bowers lay as if asleep. Scott, with his sleeping bag open, had an arm flung over Wilson.

The men gently searched the sleeping bags and clothing. They found letters and diaries and Wilson's valuable 35-pound bag of rocks.

With bowed heads the party held a memorial service. Then the tent was closed and covered with a great pile of snow. A wide hunt was made for Oates' body, but it could not be found.

On February 14, 1913, the king of England held a memorial service in St. Paul's Cathedral, London.

Amundsen had been the first to reach the South Pole. But Scott's brave race and tragic death made him a hero to the world.

Kathleen Scott made a statue of her husband in his Antarctic furs. A reminder of his steady leadership and courage, it stands in Waterloo Place, London.

But the best memorials of Scott and his companions are their carefully kept maps and records—the keys to the mystery of the great white continent.

ATLANTIC OCEAN

To South America   To Africa

ANTARCTICA

INDIAN OCEAN

South Pole

PACIFIC OCEAN

Ross Sea

To Australia

Inside the box is the part of Antarctica
that Scott explored.

- - - - - - - - Scott's route 1901–1903

———————— Scott's route 1911–1912

First Expedition, 1901-1903

1   King Edward VII Land, which Scott discovered
as he sailed along the coast of Antarctica

2   Scott was forced to turn back here on his first
attempt to reach the South Pole.

3   Scott and another man dropped into a deep
crevasse here while exploring Victoria Land.

Second Expedition, 1911-1912

4   A motor sledge fell through soft ice here as the
men were unloading the *Terra Nova*.

5   The exploring party was trapped here for four
days by heavy rain on Scott's second attempt
to reach the South Pole.